THE GREAT ALPHABET REMINDER BOOK

Story by - Ernest Boehnert

Illustrations - Rollie Bourassa

Order this book online at www.trafford.com
or email orders@trafford.com

Most Trafford titles are also available at major online book retailers.

Note for Librarians: A cataloguing record for this book is available from Library
and Archives Canada at www.collectionscanada.ca/amicus/index-e.html

Printed in Victoria, BC, Canada.

ISBN: 978-1-4269-1256-6 (sc)
ISBN: 978-1-4269-1258-0 (e-book)

*Our mission is to efficiently provide the world's finest, most comprehensive book publishing
service, enabling every author to experience success. To find out how to publish your book, your
way, and have it available worldwide, visit us online at www.trafford.com*

Trafford rev. 10/20/2009

Trafford
PUBLISHING®   www.trafford.com

North America & international
toll-free: 1 888 232 4444 (USA & Canada)
phone: 250 383 6864 ◆ fax: 812 355 4082

FOREWORD

The Great Alphabet Reminder Book is designed to assist young students in relearning and remembering the significance of the alphabet. The focus is on repetition and association of the letters in the alphabet with particular words and sounds. Many new vocabulary words will provide the young reader with the basis for remembering the alphabet letter in question. Vocabulary that may be unfamiliar to the young reader has been underlined. An explanation of these words, in terms akin to a young reader's insight, appears at the end of each story.

The Great Alphabet Reminder Book reinforces usage of the alphabet for young readers. It complements and reviews the work of the classroom instructor who is teaching the alphabet.

"A"

Albert Alligator arrived in Abletown, <u>Alabama</u>. He had come to see his relatives. They were Uncle Alvin, Aunt Ann, cousin Andy, and cousin Alice. Uncle Alvin was an <u>architect</u> and Aunt Ann was an <u>astronomer.</u> Albert's cousins were still in school. Andy wanted to be an <u>astronaut.</u> Alice had been an artist for two years already.

Albert wanted to see all the interesting things that were in Abletown. Andy took him to see the apple juice factory. Then they went to the <u>Aquatic</u> Arena to watch the exercise classes in the pool. On the way home, they went into an <u>aquarium</u> shop that had many different kinds of fish to see.

At night Albert thought about all the different things everyone would do tomorrow. First they were going to see the <u>automobile</u> <u>assembly</u> plant. Then they would watch an <u>archery</u> contest. Alice wanted Albert to see her paintings at an art display in school. Uncle Alvin was also going to take them to the Amusement Park in Abbot City.

Alabama   - a state in the United States, like provinces in Canada

Architect   - a person who draws plans for making buildings

Astronomer - a person who learns about space and the stars

Astronaut   - a person who travels in a space ship

Aquatic   - It has to do with water, like a pool and swimming

Aquarium   - a glass tank with water to keep fish in

Automobile - another name for a car

Assembly   - to put parts and things together

Archery   - shooting arrows with a bow

"B"

Bobby Beaver bit on a branch from a tree. He was helping his family build a dam to hold back the water of Blossom Brook. The beaver family needed to build a _barrier_ so the water would be deep enough to make a pond. Then they would build a beaver house to live in for the winter.

Bobby lived with his father and mother, his twin brothers Bart and Brian, and his sister Barbara. Grandpa Beaver lived with the family too. Bobby did not have a grandma anymore. One day Grandma Beaver cut down a big, _birch_ tree but it accidentally fell on her.

Bobby climbed up on the riverbank to rest because he was tired. Bobby _basked_ in the bright summer sunlight. Building a dam was hard work. He felt _drowsy_ and went to sleep. A big brown bear was eating blueberries and he saw Bobby. Suddenly, Barbara Beaver slapped the water with her _broad_, flat, tail and Bobby woke up. He was _bewildered_ and _barely_ jumped into the water in time to escape from the bear. Bobby knew he should not have been sleeping when the dam had to be built.

Barrier   - the dam is a barrier, it stops the water from going further down the river

Birch   - a tree that has white bark

Basked   - to sit and relax in the warm sunshine

Drowsy   - we feel tired and sleepy

Broad   - wide, spread out, a piece of wood might be ten centimetres wide

Bewildered   - when we do not know what is happening, we are mixed up and confused

Barely   - we get something done just in time

"C"

Conrad Cat thought he was cool. His fur was combed, his face was clean, he was warm and comfortable. His eyes were closed and he was <u>purring</u> contentedly. Conrad was curled up on the <u>windowsill</u> of Mrs. Carter's <u>cottage.</u> Conrad and Mrs. Carter lived in the city of Camwood.

Conrad was a different kind of cat. He did not like to be outside except to sniff <u>crocuses</u> in spring. Once the neighbour's <u>collie</u> almost crawled through the fence to try and catch Conrad.

Suddenly Conrad was outside! He was being entertained by a clown who had a collection of circus balloons. Conrad enjoyed chasing the balloons all over the lawn. He liked to <u>clutch</u> the balloons with his claws to make them pop and break.

All at once the clown disappeared! Conrad was now <u>surrounded</u> by many dogs that all looked like the neighbour's collie. Conrad was very frightened! He jumped high in the air and landed,with a thump, on something hard. Conrad fell on the living room coffee table - he had been dreaming.

Purring   - the soft rumbling noise a cat makes when it is happy

Windowsill - the lower part of the wall that is around a window in a house

Cottage   - a small house

Crocus   - a wild flower that is purple and blooms in spring

Collie   - a special breed or type of dog

Clutch   - to hold or grab something tightly

Surround   - to go all around or make a circle around something

"D"

David Dingo was a wild dog. Dingoes live in the desert in <u>Australia.</u> One morning David decided it would be a good day to <u>explore</u> things with his friends - Darrel, Dwayne, and Dizzy. Dizzy Dingo was called Dizzy because he couldn't walk straight.

After they had walked a while, the four young dingoes were getting hungry. Darrell found some dry desert mushrooms which they all ate. Dwayne wished that he had some <u>Dijon</u> mustard to make them taste better. Now everyone was thirsty so they all had a drink of water from a deep hole in the desert sand.

It was getting late so the four <u>adventurous</u> dingoes decided to go home. They had not <u>discovered</u> many things but they didn't want their families to be worried.

David hoped he could see and do other things in the desert on the days that he would wander about. For now he was <u>snuggled</u> down with his family in the <u>den</u> and he could only dream about <u>future</u> discovery days.

Australia   - a country that is in the southern part of the world and close to Antarctica

Explore   - to look around for things, find things, travel about

Dijon   - a type of mustard to put on a hot dog

Adventurous - to travel and see new places

Discovered   - to find something

Snuggled   - cozy, warm, and comfortable, perhaps in bed

Den   - a cave or hiding place where the dingoes lived

Future   - some time later, a tomorrow, things that will happen after a while

"E"

Edith Emu was a large bird. She looked a bit like an ostrich but a little smaller. Edith lived in <u>Australia</u>. She ate fruits, roots, and plants for food.

Edith was sad and lonely. Eleven days ago she had left her family. Edith had decided to be <u>responsible</u> for herself. She missed her brothers and sisters - Eric, Ethan, Evely, and Edna. Edith had looked everywhere but she could not find another emu. Her eyes were getting tired from looking at everything. She was so sad that her eyes were filled with tears. Edith even thought about returning home.

Edith was not watching her steps. Suddenly, she tripped, fell, and slid to the edge of the riverbank. Her head bumped against a large stone and she was <u>unconscious.</u>

Edith woke up and she could feel water falling on her. She opened her eyes. What a surprise! There was another emu throwing water at her.

"Hi",said the emu,"my name is Engelbert Emu. I saw you fall and hurt your head. I was trying to <u>revive</u> you. What is your name?"

"Edith",replied Edith.

Edith was very glad because she had found a friend.

Australia   - a country that is in the southern part of the world and close to Antarctica

Responsible - we look after ourselves, we do other things for people around us

Unconscious- if we have fainted or hurt ourselves maybe we do not know what is happening around us

Revive   - to wake up,to feel better after we have been sick or hurt

"F"

Franklin Fox laughed and laughed. His friend Felix Fox looked very funny. Franklin had been first to <u>scamper</u> along a fallen log to cross a <u>shallow</u> river. Felix followed but he lost his <u>footing</u> and fell into the mud. Felix looked like a black fox. Franklin kept on laughing while Felix washed himself in the river.

The two foxes went under a farmer's fence and walked through a forest to get to a <u>meadow.</u> This was one of Franklin' favorite places. A <u>falcon</u> flew overhead and his feathers <u>fluttered</u> in the wind. The smell of fresh flowers was everywhere. Felix and Franklin were looking for food to eat since they had not found any fish in the river.

Finally the two friends saw some fresh berries to eat. Now they could have an enjoyable feast. They quickly began to eat berries. After a short while, Felix began to laugh at his friend. Franklin has so much berry juice on his face and ears that he looked like a purple fox. Felix could now say that he had the last laugh!

Scamper   - To jump and run about happily

Shallow   - not very deep, there is not much water in the river

Footing   - where we are stepping or walking on

Meadow   - a place where grass and flowers grow; birds, butterflies, and
                insects would live there

Falcon   - a hunting bird like a hawk

Fluttered   - to move back and forth in the wind like a flag or kite

"G"

Gerald Giraffe lived in <u>Africa.</u> He was still young and not full grown. Later he would be over five <u>metres</u> tall. Gerald's tongue would even be about forty-five <u>centimetres</u> long. As an adult, Gerald would have a long <u>tufted</u> tail, a long neck, and long <u>gangly</u> legs.

Because Gerald was so tall, he had to spread his front legs apart in order to drink water or <u>graze.</u> Gerald usually ate the leaves that were found on the higher branches of the trees. It would take a great big pile of leaves to be enough food for Gerald. He would be able to eat more than a <u>gaggle</u> of geese, a group of goats, or eight giant penguins.

Gerald can also run very fast. A giraffe can take giant steps and <u>gallop</u> about forty-eight <u>kilometres</u> an hour. Yet, Gerald wouldn't be able to give a big shout or cheer at the end of a race. Giraffes are almost voiceless and cannot really make sounds like other animals do.

Africa   - a large continent or land area south of Europe and the Mediterranean Sea. There are many countries in Africa.

Metre   - a way to measure things. A door knob is about one metre in distance from the floor in a house

Centimetre - a way to measure things. A big paper clip is about one centimeter wide. It takes a hundred centimeters to make a metre

Tufted   - a tail like a lion. There is a bunch of hair at the end of the tail.

Gangly   - long, skinny, almost clumsy at times

Graze   - when animals walk around and eat grass

Gaggle   - the name for a small group of geese

Gallop   - to run very fast

Kilometre   - a way to measure things. A kilometer is one thousand metres placed side by side to make a long distance.

"H"

Hannah Hyena lived in the city of Halifax, Nova Scotia. She had been born there. That is why she was sometimes called Halifax Hannah. Her mate, Henry, had come to Halifax on a cruise ship. Henry and Hannah, along with their children, Hazel, Hilary and Howard, lived at the Halifax Zoo. The hyena family lived behind a high fence that held back the <u>humans</u> who came to the zoo.

Hannah and her family were laughing hyenas. They were always laughing because hyenas have a great sense of <u>humour</u>. The hyena family became a huge attraction because the human visitors liked to hear them laugh. The hyenas were actually telling jokes to each other.

Hyenas can learn things by watching other animals or people. One day a human visitor dropped a <u>Polaroid Camera</u> through the fence at the zoo. In a short while, the hyenas were able to take pictures of humans. They saw people with funny hats, huge dimples, horrible teeth, and bad hair days. The hyenas had great fun laughing at the funny pictures of the human visitors who came to see them. It was <u>hilarious!</u>

Humans   - another name for people

Humour   - when we laugh at funny things

Polaroid Camera   - a camera that gives you a photo shortly after you have taken a picture

Hilarious   - when something is very funny and we laugh a lot

"I"

Isabel <u>Impala</u> loved to run. She could run so fast that even lions couldn't catch her. Isabel was only about one <u>metre</u> high at her shoulders and she did not weigh very much. Isabel lived in Africa.

One day Isabel went into the city to the racehorse track. The <u>jockeys</u> were taking their horses to run a race. The horses had been trained to run behind a flag that was tied to a car. The car could easily stay ahead of the horses. The race started, the people cheered and whistled! Isabel became very excited! She jumped over the <u>guardrail</u> and easily ran past the horses and the <u>automobile</u>.

The car with the flag was back on the track for the second race, but it wouldn't start. The second race could not begin.

"We want Isabel! We want Isabel!" shouted the noisy crowd.

Isabel took the flag and raced around the track ahead of the horses. Then the track <u>officials</u> asked Isabel to be the First Starter for all the races. Now Isabel runs, the jockeys try to get their horses to catch her, and the starter automobile does not <u>pollute</u> the air.

Impala   - a small member of the deer family; these animals live in Africa.

Metre   - a way to measure things. A door knob is about one metre in
              distance from the floor in a house

Jockeys   - people who ride racehorses around a track

Guardrail   - a fence to stop people from walking on the race track

Automobile - another name for a car

Officials   - people who make sure a game or sport is played by the rules.
              In a hockey game, the official is the referee.

Pollute   - if we litter and throw garbage around. Air is polluted by car
              exhaust or smoke from a fire.

"J"

Jeremy Jackal wore his best silk shirt. It was the colour of hot pink jelly beans. He was enjoying himself at the Jamboree Jungle Entertainment Arena. The jazz band was very <u>lively.</u> Jeremy was moving and shaking like jello - he was <u>jiving.</u> His friends called him Jiving Jeremy.

Jeremy had discovered the Jamboree Jungle Entertainment Arena in January. It was a <u>nightclub.</u> One evening while he was jogging, Jeremy heard music coming from a building some distance away. Jeremy went inside the building and discovered that the Junior Jungle Band was having a <u>jam session</u> or practice. They were playing musical instruments. Jeremy was also surprised to see his friend Jennifer Jackal singing and dancing with the music.

"Hey Jeremy," said the band leader, "dance with the lady."

Jeremy replied, "I don't know how to jive."

"Well," said Jennifer, "I can show you!"

Jeremy took dance lessons until the end of July. At a dance contest, the judges decided that Jeremy was the best jive dancer in the Jamboree Jungle Entertainment Arena. Now Jeremy was famous from <u>Japan</u> to <u>Jamaica.</u>

Lively	- when we show lots of action, we are excited and noisy
Jiving	- a special way to dance People in the movie "Grease" were jiving when they danced.
Nightclub	- a place where singers, dancers, and musicians perform to entertain people
Jam session	- It is not to eat. This means that musicians get together and practice. They play their instruments and learn to play music.
Japan	-A country of islands close to Korea and China
Jamaica	-An island that is east of Mexico and south of Cuba and Florida.

"K"

Kareen Kangaroo sat in her rocking chair on the front porch. It was evening and the sun was slowly setting in Australia. Soon she would have to put her twin boys, Kenny and Karl to bed. Kareen was knitting a <u>kerchief</u> for her neighbour, Kendra Kangaroo. Kareen put a <u>knot</u> in her knitting and went indoors. She was <u>keen</u> to continue but it was now bedtime.

Kareen awoke in the middle of the night. The sky had a strange glow, like the colour of mustard and ketchup. It was a fire and Kareen knew she had to warn the neighbours! She woke up Kenny and Karl, told them to <u>warn</u> Grandpa Kangaroo and then go to the river to escape the fire. Kareen kicked and knocked on all the neighbours' doors. Soon everyone was going to the river. Even rancher Kerwin, his wife Kathleen, and their dog, King, were there.

Everyone was safe at the river except Grandpa Kangaroo. A big burning tree had fallen on Grandpa and killed him. Everybody was sad but Kareen was a <u>heroine</u> because she had saved many lives. The story of her adventure was written in the "Kimberly Korner" newspaper.

Kerchief	- a piece of cloth that women use to tie around their hair
Knot	- we make a knot to tie something like shoe laces or a ribbon on a gift box
Keen	- we want to do something very much. We might be keen to watch television instead of washing the dishes after dinner.
Warn	- we tell someone about danger or a big problem
Heroine	- a female who does something brave to help others

"L"

It was winter time. Leroy Lynx was lying on a large rock halfway up a hillside. He was looking down into the valley and watching the Lumberjack Lads practise lifting and throwing logs as far as they could. The Lumberjack Lads were the sons of the <u>lumberjacks</u> who worked in the forest. The boys were getting ready for the <u>Winter Festival.</u> Leroy thought he could easily learn to lift and toss logs. When the boys left, Leroy tried throwing logs too. It was easy and Leroy took less time than the boys to learn the throwing skills.

Next day Leroy saw the boys put their names on a long list. Later, Leroy looked at the list and added his own name as well. The list showed who had entered the log throwing contest for the Winter Festival.

A large crowd came to see the Winter Festival. Small children even stood on ladders so they could see everything. Leroy wore his lumberjack shirt and large boots. The logs that Leroy threw went a <u>further</u> distance than those of any other thrower. Leroy was the log throwing champion! The crowd loved him. He won first prize. Leroy felt proud, he was the best log-throwing lynx in the land!

Lumberjacks   - people who cut down trees in the forest

Winter Festival- games, sports, and contests that people play outdoors in the
                winter time

Further   - one distance is longer than another - you could throw a ball
                further than your friend can

"M"

It was Monday. Myrna Moose was walking alone in the forest. She had told her husband, Major Moose, to stay home. Myrna was looking for something. Myrna was about to become a mother and she was trying to find a pleasant place in the forest to give birth. After she had a nice meal of meadow grass, Myrna lay down to rest beside a maple tree. Myrna <u>dozed</u> and dreamed about a <u>manicure</u> and muffins she had once seen in a magazine.

All at once, Myrna knew that she could go no further. This spot, beside the maple tree, was going to be Myrna's <u>maternity room.</u> Soon the baby began to arrive. It was almost a matter of magic. But wait, another baby began to arrive as well. This was too much because a third baby was also born!

What a moment! Myrna was the mother of <u>triplets!</u> Major Moose had to be told. Myrna called to the magpies and meadowlarks for help. Soon the forest was <u>abuzz</u> with the news. Even the mallard ducks quacked about the new mother. Major Moose came running! All of the forest creatures wanted to see the triplets. The old maple tree would mark a special place in the forest where Myrna became the mother of three babies.

Dozed   - to get sleepy, close your eyes, and have a little nap

Manicure   - when people trim their fingernails and put nail polish on them

Maternity room - a special room in a hospital where mothers go to give birth
                        to their babies

Triplets   - when three babies are born to the same mother all on the
                     same day. The babies all have the same birthday,

Abuzz   - everyone is talking about some exciting news

"N"

Nellie <u>Nuthatch</u> was perched high up in the branches of a tree. This morning she was singing a cheerful song. Nellie was about as big as a bluebird in size. Her feathers were a grey colour. For food, Nellie ate insects, nuts, hard seeds, and berry stones.

Nellie was building a nest. Her mate, Nathan, was also helping. The nuthatch family took things from their <u>natural</u> surroundings to build a nest. They closed the opening of the nest with <u>clay</u> and only left a hole large enough to go in and out. Nellie and Nathan used the inside bark of trees and dry leaves to make a nice bed in the nest. Everything looked very <u>neat</u>. Now Nellie could lay some eggs in their new home.

Even if the north wind became cold, the nest was warm and comfortable. Soon the eggs in the nest <u>hatched.</u> The noisy babies nodded their heads and opened their mouths for food. When the babies slept, Nathan sang loudly to tell everyone that now he and Nellie were new parents.

Nuthatch	- a small grey-coloured bird The nuthatch gets its name from the way it chips open nuts with a sharp bill
Natural	- things like trees, grass, soil, and leaves that you would find outdoors in nature
Clay	- a type of soil that is found in the ground below the top soil Pieces of clay will stick together when they are wet.
Neat	- when things are clean, tidy, and all in their proper place
Hatched	- when baby birds have grown inside an egg and peck their way out of the egg shell

"O"

Olivia Owl belonged to the <u>snowy owl</u> family. Her feathers were as white as snow. Olivia was sitting very still. It was a cold winter night and the moon was shining. The night was special because it was Christmas Eve!

Olivia was very surprised because Santa's sleigh and reindeer suddenly passed overhead! Then, as she watched, a bright orange box fell from Santa's sleigh. All at once, Santa's sleigh began to travel around in circles and soon it landed close by.

"Oh dear," groaned Santa, "what am I going to do? If I don't find it, the boys and girls won't be getting any of their Christmas gifts."

Olivia decided to fly over to Santa to find out what the problem was on this Christmas Eve.

"What are you looking for Santa?" she asked.

"I've lost my Outer Orbit Direction Object." said Santa. "I use it to keep from getting lost."

"I will go back and try to find it for you," said Olivia.

Away she flew. In a short while Olivia came back with the orange box,

"Is this it?" asked Olivia, "I saw it fall from your sleigh when you passed overhead."

"Yes," said Santa, "Thank you! I have to hurry now, I have a lot of gifts to deliver."

The sleigh was soon out of sight. Olivia could now think of herself as the snowy owl that had saved Christmas.

Snowy owl   - owls that have white feathers They live in the far north of Canada.

"P"

Percy Penguin lived in <u>Antarctica</u> near the South Pole. He lived close to Probe Research Station.   People from far-away places came here to learn about Antarctica. When Percy and his friends would go to Probe Research Station, the people there would give them pancakes or apple pie.

Suddenly, in the <u>distance</u> there was a loud explosion and a fire. Percy and his friends ran over to where it had happened. A plane had crashed, the pilot was hurt, and he was in pain. The only things that had not burned were some paint cans, paper bundles, purple ropes, and plastic water pipes.

"We need to get this pilot to Probe Research Station as quickly as we can!" said Percy.

The penguins took some purple ropes and tied the pipes together to make a sleigh. They used the paper bundles to make a pillow for the pilot. Another rope was used to pull the sleigh. Next, the penguins used the paint cans for markers so the people at Probe Research Station could find where the plane had crashed. When the penguins brought the pilot to Probe Research Station, they were heroes. This time Percy and his friends were served <u>pecan</u> pie with peach-flavored ice cream as a reward.

Antarctica   - a large continent or land area at the South Pole of Earth. It is
                  very cold and there is lots of ice and snow.

Distance   - how far something is away How far is your house from the
                  school you go to?

Pecan   - a nut that looks a bit like a walnut after you take off the shell

"Q"

Queenie Quail was a <u>prairie</u> bird. She looked a bit like her cousin, Penelope Partridge. Queenie was a quiet bird, not like the ducks who were always quacking.

It was winter time and Queenie noticed that the weather was changing. The wind was blowing and it was snowing more quickly. Queenie knew that a winter storm or blizzard was coming soon. A large <u>quantity</u> of snow was already <u>drifting</u> around the trees.

Queenie looked around and saw that Quinn Rabbit and his twin sister, Quadra, were out in the <u>meadow.</u> They were walking very slowly. Quadra was limping and holding a tree branch for a walking stick. Queenie flew over to meet the twins and talk to them.

"Can you help us?" asked Quinn. My sister has a sharp porcupine <u>quill</u> in her foot. We can't walk very fast and the storm is getting worse. We won't get home in time."

The first thing Queenie did was to use her beak to pull the quill out of Quadra's foot. Then she dug her way into a snowbank to make a shelter for them all. Next, Queenie scratched the ground to find some seeds and dry berries. Three friends were all <u>huddled</u> together in the shelter. They were warm, they had food, and they were quite comfortable. Queenie and the twins could wait until the storm was over.

Prairie   - flat, dry land that you would find in western Canada or the United States

Quantity   - how much of something there is

Drifting   - the wind pushes the snowflakes around and makes big piles or drifts

Meadow   - a piece of land in the countryside where grass is growing

Quill   - a porcupine has these sharp needle-like things to protect itself.

Huddled   - to sit close beside someone

33

"R"

Ralph Reindeer was <u>residing</u> at the Red Fox Inn. He was on vacation in the city of Reston, <u>Norway</u>. This was <u>unusual</u> since reindeers who help Santa do not take holidays two weeks before Christmas. Ralph was very tired. He had <u>requested</u> a holiday and Santa told him to rest for a few days.

The <u>residents</u> of Reston were unhappy. Snow and ice had made the mail train slide off the railway tracks. The train could not get to Reston and Christmas mail was not getting delivered. Rahls, the mailman, was feeling very sad.

"Tell me Ralph, how can I get the mail?" Rahls asked. "The children need to get their letters to Santa before Christmas."

"You can ride on my back," said Ralph, "I can jump over the big snowbanks and get you to the mail train."

Reindeer that live at the North Pole gradually learn the magic to leap high in the air just like the reindeer that pull Santa's sleigh. That is why Ralph could easily go over the big snowbanks. Soon they were at the mail train and in a little while all the Christmas mail was at the post office in Reston.

Ralph <u>decided</u> it was time to return to the North Pole and help Santa with the letters that would be coming from the children of Reston, Norway.

Residing   - where we live, our home

Norway   - a country in northern Europe

Unusual   - not what we always do, something is different

Requested   - when we ask for something

Residents   - the people who live in a town, city or some other place

Decided   - we make up our minds to do something

"S"

Sylvia Swan and her husband, Sydney, spent their summer at a lake in northern Saskatchewan. Sylvia's sister, Susan, and her mate, Sheldon, also lived there. Many other swans shared the lake.

One sunny, September, day the swans were sitting on the shore of the lake talking about flying south for the winter. Suddenly, they were scattering and scurrying everywhere! Sly Fox wanted to have swans for supper. Even though all the birds escaped, Susan Swan had a severely injured foot. Sly Fox had bit her!

Susan was not able to stand on her sore foot. She was very worried. Susan could not run fast enough to become airborne in order to fly. All the other swans left to fly south, only Sylvia and Sydney stayed to help Susan. Soon the weather got colder and then it began to snow. Next day, the lake was frozen solid. Then Sydney had a smart idea!

"Let's have Susan stand between us and put one of her wings on each of us," said Sydney, "we can run on the ice to get airborne. When we are up in the sky, Susan can flap her wings and we'll fly south."

The plan was a success. The three swans were finally on their way south to be with friends and family.

Saskatchewan - a province in western Canada

Scattering   - to run away in all directions

Scurrying   - to run here and there or back and forth

Severely   - a bad situation, something is very serious

Airborne   - to be in the air and fly like a bird or plane

"T"

Tambu Tiger lived in the <u>jungles</u> of <u>India.</u> He was only ten weeks old, he was lost and all alone. <u>Terrible</u> hunters had killed his mother and Tambu had run away. Tambu was very hungry. It was Tuesday and he had not eaten for two days. He would have taken a bite of a tomato, a turnip, or even a <u>taco</u> in order to get something to eat.

Tambu travelled to the edge of a lake. The water was very clear. It looked as if Tambu had found a tiger-twin because of his <u>reflection</u> in the water. Tambu tried to touch noses but, SPLASH he fell into the lake! The little tiger splashed, twisted, and turned. He sounded like three cats in a tub of hot water.

Teesan and his friend, Trahdoo, were standing on the lakeshore fishing. They heard Tambu and pulled him out of the water. The little tiger followed the boys back to their home in the jungle. Tambu stayed in the village and all the people liked him. He ate tomatoes, turnips, lettuce, and carrots. Tambu became a <u>vegetarian</u> tiger and lived in the village for many years.

Jungles   - places in the world where there is lots of sunshine, rain, and no
               cold winters so many trees grow there

India   - a country that is north of the Indian Ocean. Mount Everest, the
               tallest mountain in the world, is in India.

Terrible   - if something or someone is bad or evil

Taco   - a thin-baked crust of bread, folded like an envelope
               Meat,cheese,and vegetables are put inside to eat.

Reflection   - when we look in the mirror we see our image or reflection

Vegetarian   - people or animals that do not eat meat

"U"

Uda Unicorn lived in an <u>enchanted</u> forest. The sky was always blue. It was unknown if dark clouds had ever been seen where Uda lived. The butterflies in this magic forest were the colours of the rainbow.

Unicorns look like ponies except for the magic horn on their foreheads. This magic horn lets unicorns do a number of things other animals are unable to do. Unicorns like Uda, can heal a person's injuries by touching the sore spot with their horns. If you are not sure that a wish will come true, hold on to the horn of a unicorn, say your wish, and it will happen. If you <u>tumble</u> or fall, a unicorn can lift you up by just pointing its horn in your direction.

If unicorns know that you are sad, they will try to make you happy. By shaking her head, Uda could cause many shiny stars to fall around you and brighten your day. When you want to travel fast, go for a ride on a unicorn. Unicorns can travel four times faster than a pony. Their feet will hardly touch the ground or make a sound.

Unicorns are also able to stop time. For example, you would be <u>unaware</u> of when a church bell <u>chimed</u>, clocks would keep ticking but the hands would not be moving. There would be more time for children to play outdoors.

We also know that unicorns watch over children when they sleep. Unicorns always make sure that the dreams of children are in colour. With Uda's help, dreams will never have an unhappy ending.

Enchanted   - a magic place

Tumble   - if we trip or fall

Unaware   - we do not know something

Chimed   - if bells ring or make a sound

"V"

Vanessa Vulture was flying over the <u>desert</u> valley where she lived. Her <u>vision</u> was very good and she could see a <u>variety</u> of things from above. She saw vehicles like trucks hauling vegetables, vanilla ice cream wagons, vacuum salesmen, and violin repairmen in cars. Often though, the desert was <u>vacant.</u> It was very quiet with no people or voices in a conversation.

Vanessa was not a pretty bird. Her feathers were not soft like velvet. She looked like a turkey that could fly. Sometimes <u>vultures</u> are called turkey vultures. Vanessa and her vulture friends did some valuable work for Mother Nature. When animals died in the desert, the vultures were provided with food. They cleaned up the remains of animals and this prevented germs from spreading.

Vanessa saw a car stop on the highway. The driver, Vince Vonda, his wife, Veera, and their small son, Vernon got out of the car. The parents did not notice that Vernon had wandered away. From high in the sky, Vanessa could see the boy. Vanessa flew down and gently picked up Vernon. She held the boy carefully, flew over to his parents, and set him down. The family waved goodbye when Vanessa flew up into the sky. They would tell everyone that Vanessa had saved Vernon.

Desert — places where there is very little rain, it is hot and dry, and not many plants grow there

Vision — how well we can see with our eyes

Variety — many things, all the vegetables in a salad would be a variety

Vacant — empty, not much is there, lots of space

Vultures — large birds that look like turkeys and eat the remains of dead animals

 "W"

Walter Weasel was walking in the forest on a sunny day in October. Walter was thinking about his favorite food, eating <u>waffles</u> with warm maple syrup, in the winter time.

Walter went past a waving <u>willow</u> bush. A cold wind blew over him. He <u>wrinkled</u> his nose and <u>shivered.</u> Next, Walter saw a hive of bees putting more wax over their honey supply. Soon Walter went past an old hollow log and a strong wind whistled through it. The sky grew dark and the air was cold when grey clouds passed in front of the sun. At the edge of the forest, Walter saw that the sheep in Farmer White's pasture seemed to be wearing more wool.

"What does all this mean?" asked Walter. "I thought about waffles in winter, the wind was cold, the bees needed more wax, the wind whistled, clouds covered the sun, and the sheep had more wool."

Walter sat on a log to think about things for a while. Then he had an idea about what everything meant.

"I know!" he said, "Mr. Winter is telling me that he is going to come early this year. I will go and tell all the forest animals to get ready for winter."

Walter told everyone in the forest about his adventures. When the winter came, all the animals had enough food and a warm place to live until spring came.

Waffles   - breakfast food that is like pancakes but they are baked differently

Willow   - a bushy tree that does not grow very tall

Wrinkled   - to wriggle one's nose from side to side

Shivered   - we shake when we are cold

"X"

Xtrons are everywhere. They live where you do not expect them to be. For example, they might be sitting in a box next to an exercise machine or beside an extension phone. Important xtrons might have names that are special such as Trexda, Extolo, or Troxa. We should know that xtrons are not real. They only exist in our dreams and imagination.

Xtrons try to help little boys and girls. They look a bit like old teddy bears. Xtrons have extra-soft, large, feet so they can creep up quietly on bad ideas and scare them away. The xtrons get very excited when they do this! An <u>x-ray</u> would show that xtrons are almost completely <u>hollow</u> inside. This is so they can collect and keep good thoughts from happy people and give them to boys and girls that are sad. Xtrons also have very large ears. This helps them to be able to listen well as people explain why they are unhappy.

Because xtrons have very large eyes, xtrons are able to look deep inside little children to find out why they are not filled with happy thoughts. You would expect xtrons to have very large hearts and this is true. Xtrons can then <u>express</u> lots of love for everyone. Xtrons always bring good luck to people, especially children.

X-ray   - a machine that is used in a hospital to take a picture of the inside of a person's body

Hollow   - if something is empty, nothing is inside A drum that is used in a musical band is hollow inside.

Express   - if we tell or show someone our ideas or how we feel, we are expressing ourselves

"Y"

Yeremy Yak lived in <u>Tibet.</u> Yaks look like cows and they have long shaggy hair to keep them warm. It was winter time in Tibet and snow covered the land.

Yeremy was a young yak and he was bored. What could a yak do in winter time? He certainly could not sail a <u>yacht</u> or do <u>yoga</u>. One day Yeremy saw people on television and they were playing winter sports. Yeremy had a great idea!

"Say", he said, "my animal friends could organize a winter carnival! I'm going to talk to everyone about it."

The mayor thought the idea was silly but the young animals yelled and jumped for joy when they heard the news. Soon everyone was helping to get things ready. The winter carnival was going to be a busy day!

The small animals made snow angels and snowmen. <u>Adults</u> built snow houses and carved ice <u>sculptures.</u> Animals that liked to run played soccer. Some animals slid down the hills on their tummies. Last of all, Yeremy and his friends jumped into the polar pool for a winter dip in icy water. At the end of the day everybody went home tired and happy.

"I really enjoyed myself." said Yeremy to his friends, "Next winter we will <u>organize</u> a bigger and better winter carnival."

Tibet   - a country that is located north of China

Yacht   - a sailboat or a large motorboat

Yoga   - a special kind of exercises that help people stay healthy

Adults   - people that are grown up and are no longer children or teenagers

Sculptures - figures that are carved out of wood, stone, or some other material

Organize   - we have someone do a certain job, sort out things, or write out
                   directions

"Z"

Zeke Zebra lived in <u>Africa.</u> He knew many of the animals that were there and he could greet them by their first names. Everyone was <u>amazed</u> because it was a puzzle to the other animals who could not remember names. Zeke was a lively zebra. Sometimes for a razzle-dazzle trick he would turn the nozzle of a fire hose on everybody. Zeke could even waltz a few steps. The <u>Zulu</u> natives often thought that Zeke was a bit crazy. Zeke was glad he did not live in a zoo or he would not have been able to do all these funny things. One day, Zeke was surprised when an old friend called to him.

"Hey there, you <u>zany</u> zebra, how are you?" asked Zark Zeedom, the circus <u>ringmaster.</u>

"I'm fine," said Zeke, "what are you doing here?"

"I want people to see animals in Africa instead of at the circus." replied Zark, "Your Aunt Zelda told me you could help."

"That's great," replied Zeke, "I know lots of animals."

Zeke and Zark only had tourists come to visit on Tuezday, Wednezday, and Thurzday as zebra write those days. Zeke was very glad to be helping his old circus friend.

Africa   - a large continent or land area south of Europe and the
                 Mediterranean Sea. There are many countries in Africa.

Amazed   - if we are very surprised

Zulu   - native people of Africa

Zany   - being silly or funny

Ringmaster   - the person who tells an audience about the different acts in a
                 circus

Printed in the United States
By Bookmasters